Jaguar E-Type

by Julie Wilson

AXIS education

Acknowledgements

Photographs © Jaguar Cars and Wieck Media Services Inc

Copyright © Axis Education 2007

First published in Great Britain by Axis Education Ltd

ISBN 978-1-84618-090-3

Axis Education
PO Box 459
Shrewsbury
SY4 4WZ

Email: enquiries@axiseducation.co.uk

www.axiseducation.co.uk

Printed by The Cromwell Press, Trowbridge, Wiltshire.

This is a Jaguar.

It is an E-Type.

It first came out in 1961.

An E-Type Jaguar.

The E-Type is beautiful.

At first Jaguar came up with a few designs.

One design was chosen.

It was tested on the M1.

One design was chosen.

The E-Type could go at 150 miles per hour.

That is the same as 214 kilometres per hour.

It was the fastest car ever.

The fastest car ever.

Sir William Lyons began Jaguar.

He made race cars at first.

He made the C-Type and the D-Type.

The E-Type was a road car.

A Jaguar racing car.

Sir William Lyons was proud of the E-Type.

When it was ready, he showed it at the 1961 Geneva Motor Show.

People loved it.

It was just what drivers wanted in the early 1960s.

It looked great.

It had glamour.

Pop stars and footballers bought them.

The E-Type in Geneva.

Over 70,000 E-Types were made.

They were made over 14 years.

The last one was made in 1975.

14 years of the E-Type.

70,000 were made.

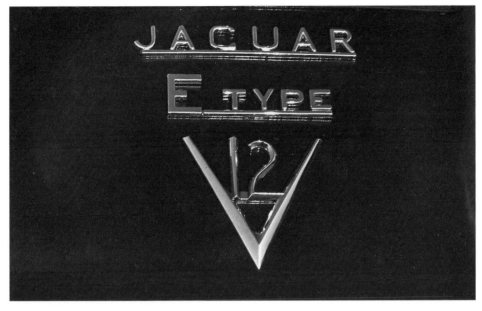

You know it's a Jaguar.

The E-Type's handling has always been good.

It has always been smooth.

It feels comfortable.

Good handling!

There were three kinds of E-Type engine.

They were the 3.8, the 4.2 and the 5.3.

The car cost £2,097 in 1961.

That was half the price of an Aston Martin or

Ferrari.

£2,097 at the time!

The bonnet is long.

The body is curvy.

It looks great.

Long bonnet and curvy body.

There are two kinds of E-Type.

There is the coupe.

There is the roadster.

You can put the top down on the roadster.

Both cars look good.

Two kinds of E-Type.

The nose is low.

The driver is low.

It is a smart ride.

It is exciting.

Exciting!

Jaguar is famous.

Its logo is famous.

Its logo is a fast cat.

JAGUAR

A fast cat.

This is an old E-Type advert.

It is from the US.

It shows the coupe and the roadster.

The cars look modern!

A modern car.

Good for racing.

A proud car.

Jaguar has made cars for years.

The E-Type is still a popular classic car.

Some owners have made websites about the E-Type.

Some have written books about it.

There are lots of Jaguar clubs to join.

Jaguar over the years.

They loved the E-Type in the US.

Many people bought them.

People still like them.

The E-Type is famous all over the world.

Popular then and now.

The E-Type is a classy car.

It is also a fun car.

It is a Jaguar.

A classy car.

Technical specification – Jaguar E-Type

Make	Jaguar
Model	E-Type
Engine size	3781cc
Top speed	150mph (214kph)
Acceleration	0 to 62mph (0 to 100kph) in 6.7 seconds
Fuel tank capacity	63.6 litres
Price	£2,097 in 1961 (on Ebay now for £22,500!)
Weight	1234kg
Transmission	4/5 speed manual
Wheelbase	2438mm

Glossary

acceleration	how fast the car speeds up
bonnet	the front of the car
capacity	how much petrol the engine can hold
cc (cubic centimetres)	a measure of engine capacity
classy	posh, stylish
coupe	a car with a fixed roof, two doors, two or four seats and usually a sloping back
curvy	rounded, wavy
exciting	thrilling; not boring!
handling	the way the car responds to the driver
kg (kilogram)	a measure of weight (just over two pounds)
kph	kilometres per hour
litre	a measure of liquid (just under two pints)
logo	the company badge
manual	done by hand
mm (millimetre)	a small measure of length: 10mm = 1cm (centimetre)
mph	miles per hour
per	for every
popular	liked by a lot of people
production car	car made in a factory
racing car	a Formula 1 car, for example
roadster	a car whose roof comes down
transmission	another word for gearbox
wheelbase	the distance between the front and rear wheels